This book belongs to .... Aged ....

It was given to me by ....

on the ..../........................./...................

Chapters

Chapter One

Water Safety

Water Safety

The key to a safe and enjoyable day's fishing is a healthy respect for the waterside and fishing environment. Remember to keep the following in mind when you are learning to fly fish:

• Always wear sunglasses or safety glasses when fly fishing to protect your eyes from sharp hooks.

• Wear a lifejacket or buoyancy aid when fishing.

• Never fly fish close to overhead power cables.

• Take care on the riverbank or lakeside - it can be slippery when wet.

• Never fly fish in a thunderstorm - a carbon fly rod can attract lightning!

• Wear waterproof sunscreen on bright days to protect you from sunburn.

• Always go fishing with a responsible adult.

• Always wash your hands carefully after you have been fishing.

Following the above rules will ensure you learn to fly fish in a safe and enjoyable environment.

Tight Lines & Be Safe!

Chapter Two

The Trout Family

The Trout Family

Trout are usually found in cool, clear rivers, streams and lakes. There are a number of different species and sub-species of trout found throughout the world. They are found naturally throughout Europe, Northern Asia and North America and were introduced to Australia and New Zealand by 19th Century British anglers. Some of the most common species are:

Brown Trout

The Brown Trout is native to Europe and Asia and has been introduced successfully to North and South America, Australia and New Zealand.

Brook Trout

A member of the Char family, the Brook Trout is native to North America and can be found mainly in streams and rivers through the eastern part of the country.

Rainbow Trout

The Rainbow Trout is native to North America. This very popular fish can be found in rivers, streams and lakes around the world.

Cutthroat Trout

The Cutthroat Trout is native to North America and can be found in streams and rivers throughout the western part of the United States.

Chapter Three

The Lifecycle of the Trout

The Lifecycle of the Trout

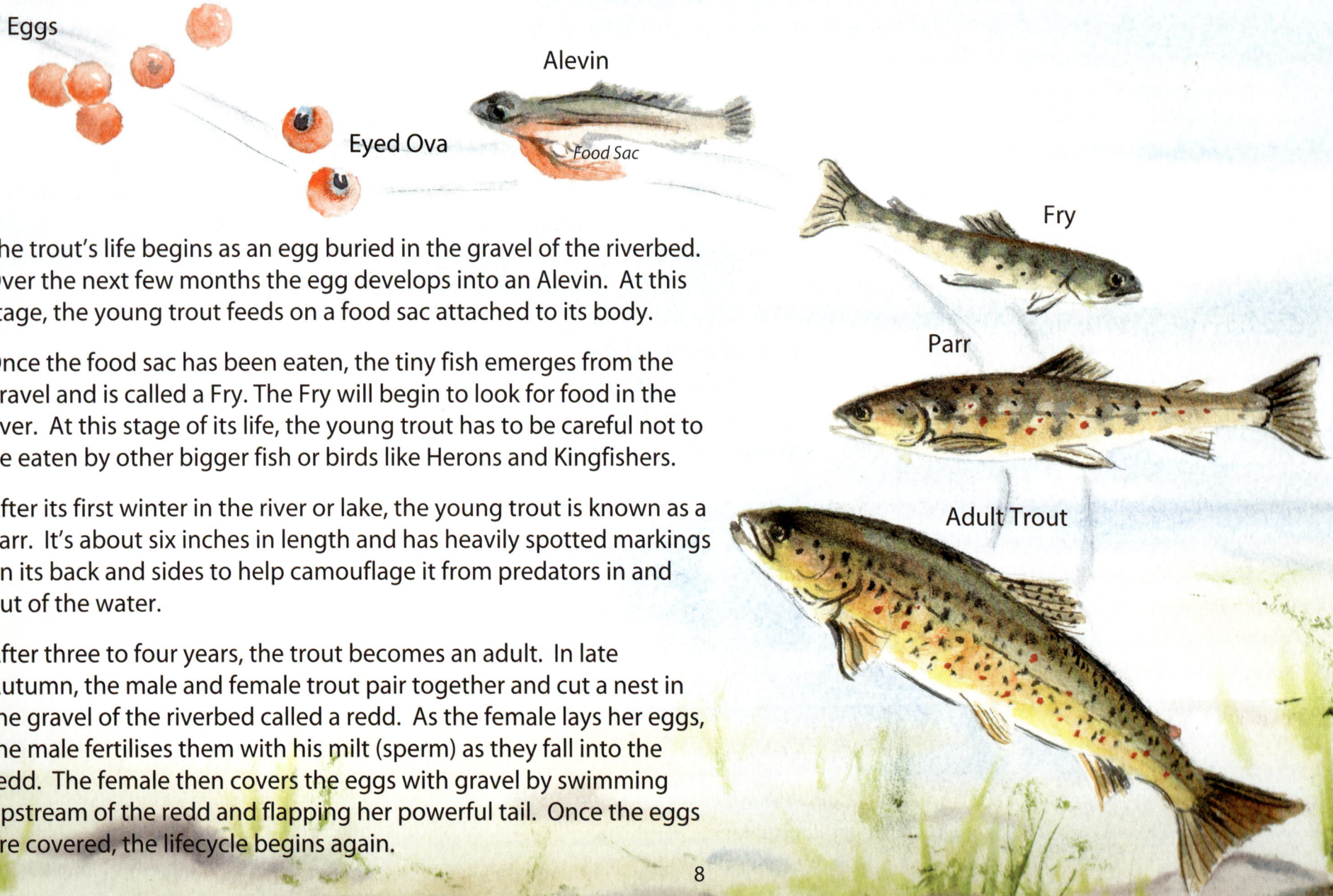

Eggs

Eyed Ova

Alevin

Food Sac

Fry

Parr

Adult Trout

The trout's life begins as an egg buried in the gravel of the riverbed. Over the next few months the egg develops into an Alevin. At this stage, the young trout feeds on a food sac attached to its body.

Once the food sac has been eaten, the tiny fish emerges from the gravel and is called a Fry. The Fry will begin to look for food in the river. At this stage of its life, the young trout has to be careful not to be eaten by other bigger fish or birds like Herons and Kingfishers.

After its first winter in the river or lake, the young trout is known as a Parr. It's about six inches in length and has heavily spotted markings on its back and sides to help camouflage it from predators in and out of the water.

After three to four years, the trout becomes an adult. In late Autumn, the male and female trout pair together and cut a nest in the gravel of the riverbed called a redd. As the female lays her eggs, the male fertilises them with his milt (sperm) as they fall into the redd. The female then covers the eggs with gravel by swimming upstream of the redd and flapping her powerful tail. Once the eggs are covered, the lifecycle begins again.

Chapter Four

The Anatomy of a Trout

The Anatomy of a Trout

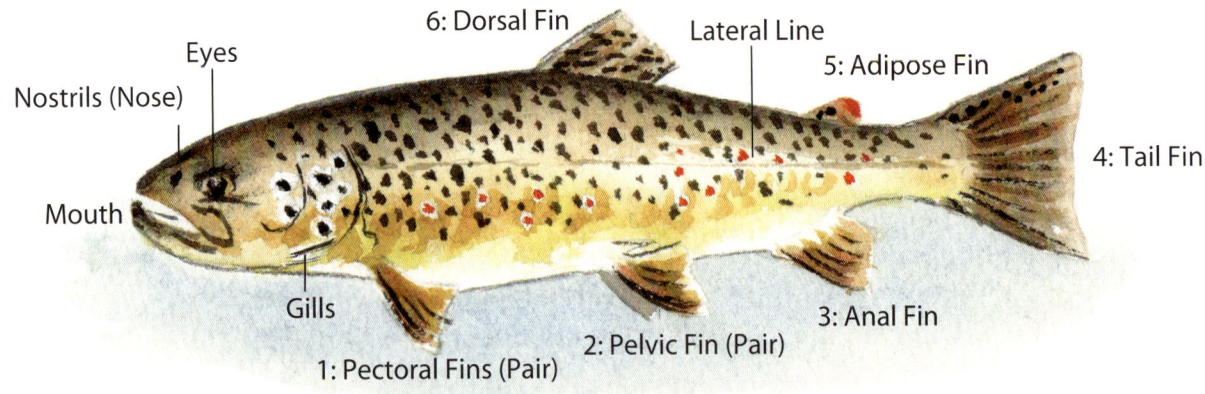

6: Dorsal Fin

Eyes

Lateral Line

5: Adipose Fin

Nostrils (Nose)

Mouth

4: Tail Fin

Gills

1: Pectoral Fins (Pair)

2: Pelvic Fin (Pair)

3: Anal Fin

Trout are cold-blooded animals and belong to the same group of fish as salmon, grayling and char. They have a backbone and use fins to manoeuvre in the water. A trout has four single fins and two sets of paired fins. By moving its fins, the trout can maintain its position in strong currents as well as move quickly to catch food or avoid danger. Almost all fins have a function:

1. The Pectoral Fins: Located under the gill covers, the trout has a pair of pectoral fins which allows the fish to balance, steer, stop and manoeuvre in the water.

2. The Pelvic Fins: The pelvic fins are located on the trout's belly, directly under the dorsal fin. A trout has a pair of pelvic fins and like the pectoral fins, allow the fish to balance, steer, stop and hover in the water.

3. The Anal Fin: The anal or ventral fin is located just behind the fish's anus and works in tandem with the dorsal fin to keep the trout upright and prevent it from rolling over onto its side.

4. The Tail Fin: Also known as the caudal fin, this is the largest fin of the trout and is used to supply the main power to allow the trout to move forward. This powerful fin can generate tremendous thrust to allow the fish to hold position in very strong currents or move quickly to find food or avoid predators.

5. The Adipose Fin: The adipose fin is a soft fleshy fin situated between the dorsal and the tail fin. The adipose fin is the only fin that has no effect on how the trout controls its movement in the water.

6. The Dorsal Fin: The dorsal fin is located on the trout's back. Its main function is to stabilise the trout. The dorsal fin works in partnership with the anal fin to keep the fish upright and prevent it rolling over onto its side.

As well as fins, Trout also have:

Eyes: A trout has very good eyesight and can recognise colour and shade. The trout's eyes are located on the side of its head. As well as binocular vision where both eyes focus on an object, the trout also has monocular vision which allows each eye to focus on different objects at the same time - very helpful for finding food and avoiding danger.

A Mouth: Like humans, a trout uses its mouth not only for eating food, but also for breathing - see gills. The trout draws its food into its mouth before swallowing into its stomach.

Gills: A trout breathes by drawing water into its mouth and over its gills. The gills trap tiny bubbles of oxygen, which are dissolved into the bloodstream through tiny blood vessels. When the trout opens and closes its mouth, it pumps water over the gills to keep a constant supply of clean, oxygenated water to allow it to breathe.

Nostrils: Much like our nostrils, these two tiny holes on the trout's snout allow the fish to smell. Trout have a very good sense of smell - in fact would you believe each nostril is covered in over 400,000 odour-sensing cells!

A Lateral Line: The lateral line runs along the side of the trout and is a series of special cells that sense vibration in the water to warn of danger or the presence of food outwith its field of vision.

Heron

The Heron is a very skilful and patient angler.
It will stand motionless for long periods of
time before quickly dipping its head under
the water to catch small fish.

Chapter Five

What do Trout Eat?

What Do Trout Eat?

A trout's main food consists of insects in the water called invertebrates. An invertebrate is an animal with no backbone. Although they will happily eat land-based invertebrates that fall into the water, trout feed heavily on tiny aquatic insects in rivers, streams and lakes around the world. Knowing which insects are in the rivers, streams and lakes and at what stage of their lifecycle the trout are feeding on them, is an important part of being a fly fisher.

Each insect starts life as an egg laid in the water by an adult fly. The egg develops into a nymph or larva and grows underwater before going through a change called metamorphosis. At some point during the metamorphosis the insect rises to the surface and 'hatches' out of the water as an air-breathing adult insect. Depending on the type of insect, the adult can look completely different from the nymph or larva. The insect then flies off the water and looks for other newly-hatched flies to breed with. After mating, the female insect returns to the water to lay her eggs and starts the lifecycle all over again.

As the insect develops under the surface and right to the point that the female returns to the water to lay her eggs, trout feed heavily on a large range of water-based insects.

The four main insect groups of interest to us as fly fishers are....

1: Mayfly Family

Adult Dun Mayfly

Egg-laying Mayfly Spinner

Mayfly Nymph

Eggs

2: Caddisfly Family

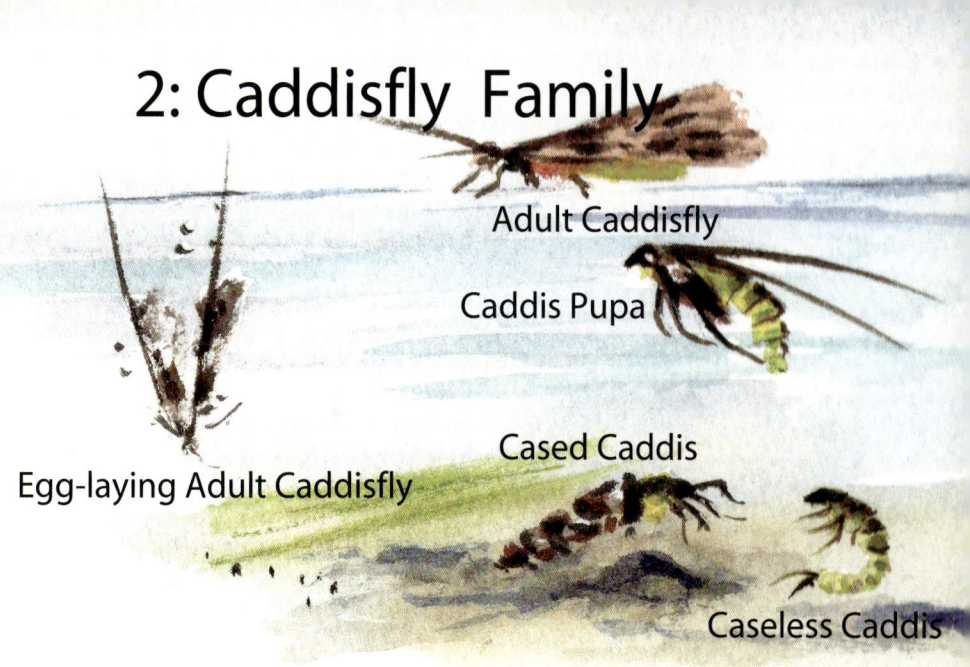

Adult Caddisfly

Caddis Pupa

Egg-laying Adult Caddisfly

Cased Caddis

Caseless Caddis

3: Midge Family

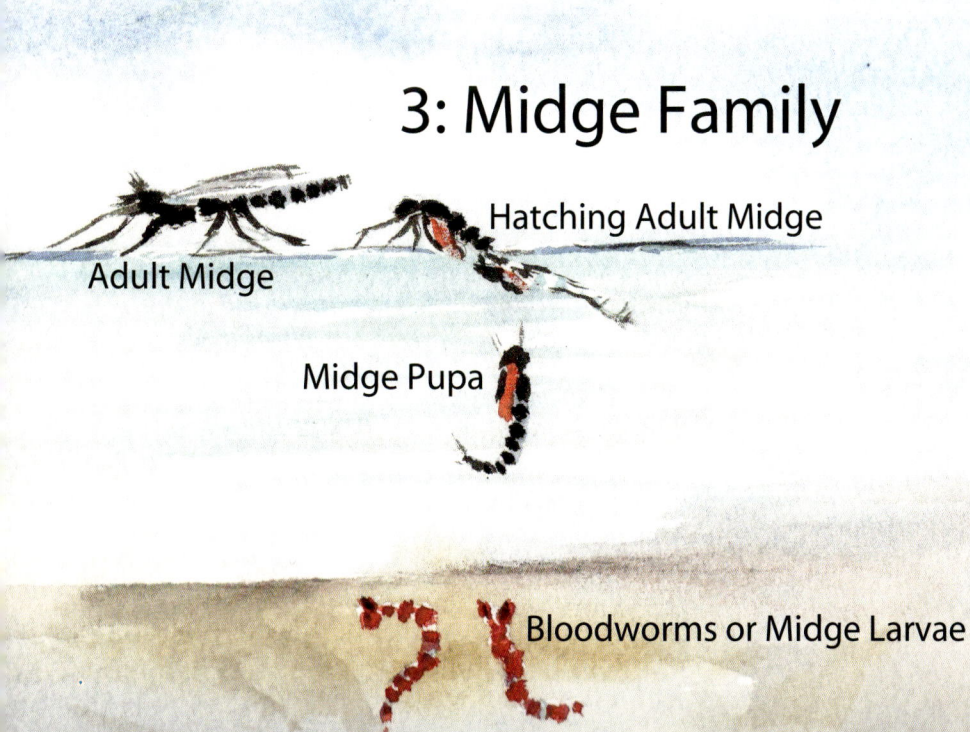

Adult Midge

Hatching Adult Midge

Midge Pupa

Bloodworms or Midge Larvae

4: Stonefly Family

Adult Stonefly

Stonefly Nymph

1. Mayflies: Known scientifically as Ephemeroptera, this group of flies are well-known to the fly fisher as a food source for trout. The mayfly nymph is easily recognised by its three tails. The adult fly has one set of large wings and one set of small wings. As adult flies they have a short life-span of only a few days. They can be found in large numbers on both rivers and lakes around the world and the mayfly is the only insect to have two parts to the adult lifecycle.

2. Caddisflies: Known scientifically as Trichoptera, the larvae of the Caddisfly either lives free in the water or makes a protective case, usually out of sticks or stones, to protect them from predators. The hatched adult fly has two sets of wings that fold like a tent when at rest. Most types of Caddisfly are normally found on rivers and lakes with clean, well-oxygenated water.

3. Midge Flies: There are many different types of midge fly. One of the most common is the non-biting midge, which is known scientifically as Chironomids and look similar in size and appearance to mosquitoes. The midge is found in vast numbers in lakes and stillwaters and is a great food-source for trout throughout the insect's lifecycle. Trout feed heavily on these invertebrates during the larva (bloodworm), pupa and adult stage.

4. Stoneflies: Known scientifically as Plecoptera, Stoneflies are mainly found in clean rivers and streams with stony bottoms. The adult fly has two tails and two sets of large wings that lie flat along the insect's back when at rest. (The name Plecoptera comes from the Greek words "pleco" meaning folded and "ptera" meaning wing). Although they often have two large sets of wings, they are not renowned fliers and tend to stay close to the ground hiding in the undergrowth.

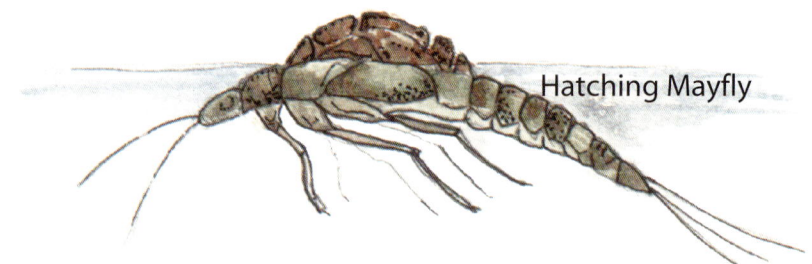

Hatching Mayfly

Chapter Six

How to Tie a Fly

How to Tie a Fly

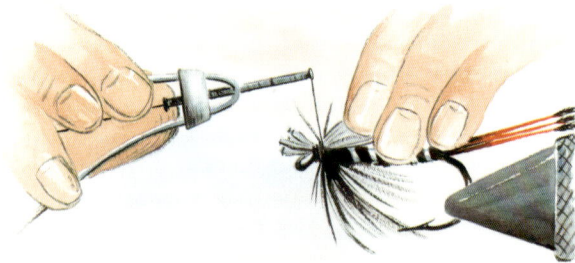

Once we know what insects the trout are feeding on, we can then tie up an artificial fly to fool the fish into thinking that it is actually a real insect it would like to eat. An important factor to consider when fishing for trout is to try and 'match the hatch' - in other words to make the artificial fly look as much as possible like the emerging or hatching insect the trout are feeding on.

Each fly is tied onto a metal hook with a very sharp point to hold the fish once it's hooked. Depending on the insect being imitated, a selection of natural materials like feathers from birds, fur and hair from animals, as well as man-made materials are tied onto the hook to copy the appearance of the particular insect.

The hook is held in a fly tying vice as various layers of material are bound onto the hook using thread dispensed from a bobbin. Each layer of material is secured by wrapping the thread around the hook several times then finished off with a small spot of varnish or glue. The last stage of construction is tying-off the thread at the head of the fly. This can be done by hand or by using a device called a whipped finish tool.

Some of the most well-known trout flies are.....

Black Buzzer/Midge Pupa

Black Zulu

Stewart Spider

Pheasant Tail Nymph

Partridge & Orange

March Brown

Greenwells Glory

Crane Fly

Damsel Nymph

Goosander

The Goosander is another very good angler. By
diving under the water, this bird feeds heavily on
small fish in rivers and lakes throughout the fishing
world. Due to its appetite for young fish, this bird is
not the trout fisherman's best friend!

Chapter Seven

Basic Knots

Basic Fishing Knots

Before we start fishing there are two basic knots that every trout fisher should learn - the Half Blood Knot and the Water Knot. The Half Blood Knot is used to connect the artificial fly to the leader, which in turn connects to the fly line - see page 25. The Water Knot is used to connect two pieces of leader material together, and to attach additional flies to the leader - known as droppers.

Half Blood Knot

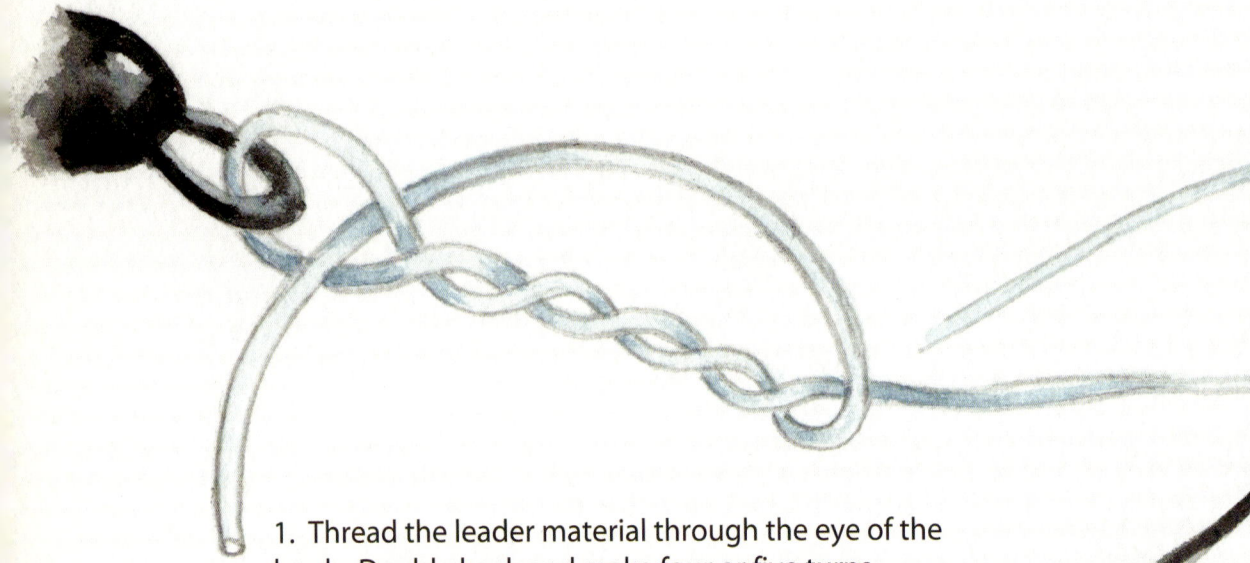

Water Knot

Half Blood Knot

1. Thread the leader material through the eye of the hook. Double back and make four or five turns around the main line.

2. Thread the line through the first loop above the eye, then pass the end through the big loop as shown.

3. Holding the end of the leader material, pull the knot tight against the eye of the hook.*

Water Knot

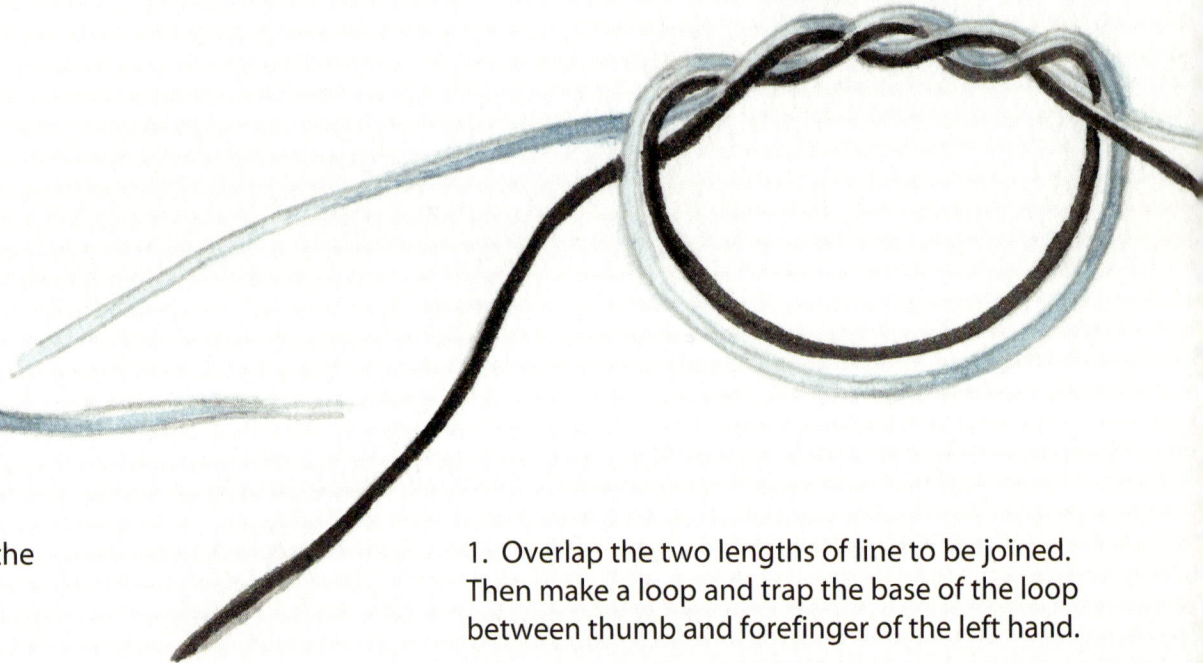

1. Overlap the two lengths of line to be joined. Then make a loop and trap the base of the loop between thumb and forefinger of the left hand.

2. With the right hand, wrap the two lengths of line through the main loop four times.

3. Moisten and draw tight*. Clip ends if required.

*A great tip is to always lubricate the knot with a small amount of saliva before pulling tight to reduce friction and retain maximum strength in the knot.

Chapter Eight

Basic Fly Casting

Basic Fly Casting

In the last few chapters we have learned how to be safe when we are fishing, learned about what insects trout feed on and how to tie an artificial fly to look like the natural insect. It's now time to learn how to present the fly to the fish by learning how to cast with a fly rod.

When fly fishing for trout, the angler casts the artificial fly out across the water using a fly rod. The fly is attached to a very thin, clear material called a leader. The leader is then connected to a fly line which runs freely through the rings of the fly rod. The angler uses the fly rod to move the fly line back and forward in the air until the fly line, leader and fly is cast out across the water.

There are two basic casts to learn before we can catch trout on a fly rod - the overhead cast and the roll cast. Both casts will present the fly out and across the water to the waiting trout. Before we look at each one, let's take a closer look at what tackle we need to learn to cast........

Fly Rod: Most modern trout fly rods are between 8ft-10ft in length and are made from a material called carbon fibre. The rod flexes with the weight of the fly line to propel the artificial fly towards the direction of the trout. Each rod has a set of rod rings to allow the line to move freely when casting, a reel seat to hold the fly reel, and a cork handle to grip the rod.

Reel: The reel attaches to the rod below the cork handle and stores the fly line. Each reel has a drag system to control the strong runs of the trout once hooked. If the fish is fighting hard, the drag can be set so the fish has to use more energy to pull line from the reel. This will tire the fish out more quickly and make it easier to land.

Fly Line: In fly casting, the weight of the fly line carries the artificial fly out and above the water. The weight of the line has to be balanced to the rod to allow the best presentation of the fly to the trout. Fly lines can either float on the water surface or sink at various speeds to take the fly to a depth that the fish are feeding.

Leader: The leader is a thin, clear material that connects the fly to the end of the fly line. Depending on fishing technique, the leader can vary in length from 9ft to 20ft. Leader material is available in various breaking strains and should never be discarded by the river or lakeside. Discarded line should be cut into short lengths before disposal at home to avoid birds and animals getting tangled up in it.

Eye Protection: It is very important to wear some form of eye protection when fly casting to protect your eyes from the very sharp hook of the artificial fly. When casting, the fly can sometimes come close to your head and as a result safety glasses or sunglasses MUST be worn at all times to guard your eyes from any contact with the hook.

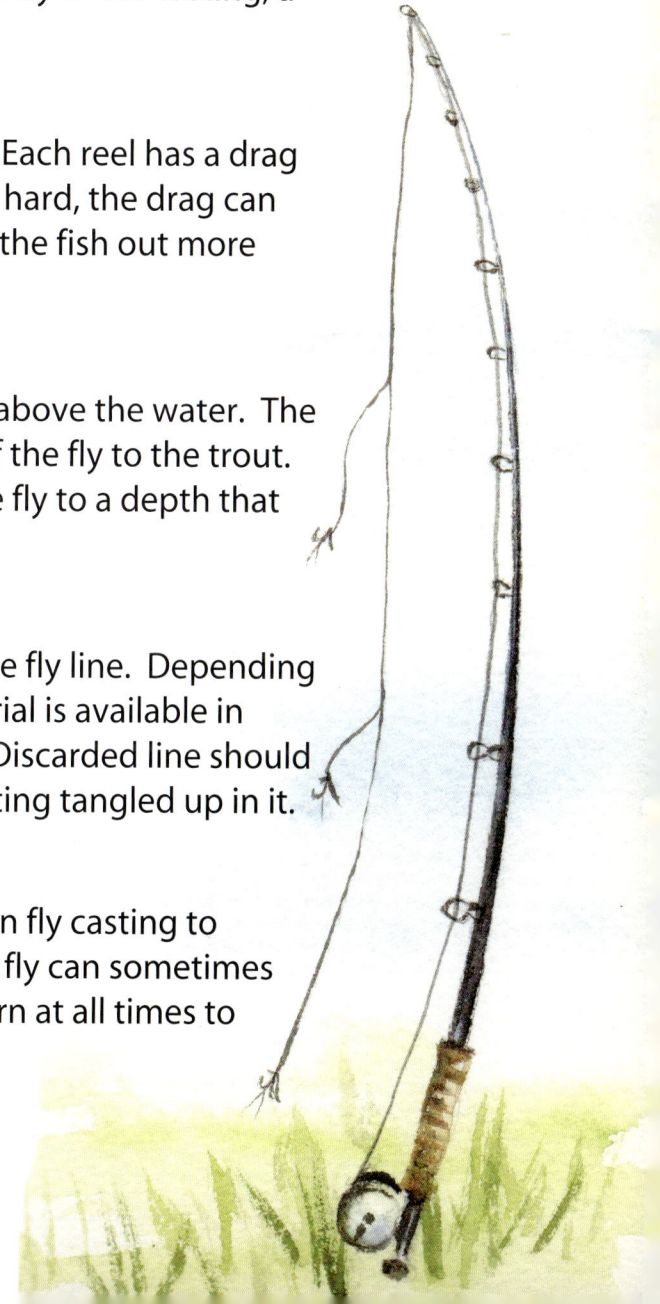

Basic Overhead Cast

1. Start by holding the rod in your favoured hand, with the fly line straight and the rod tip touching the water.

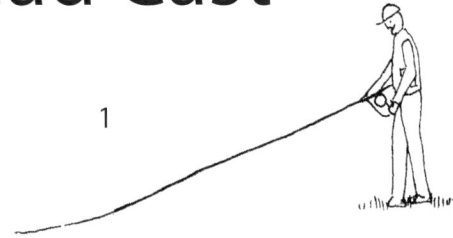

2. Begin lifting the rod tip through the clockface, making sure to accelerate smoothly upwards and backwards.

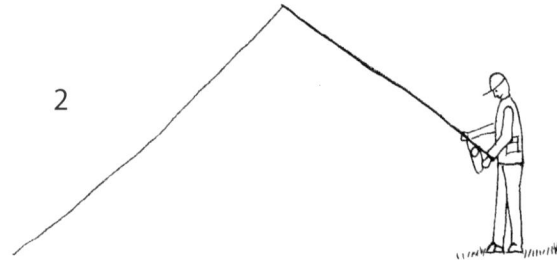

3. Continue the smooth acceleration until the rod has just passed the 12 o'clock position and the line is moving over the rod tip.

4. Keeping the rod in the same position, count out 1-2-3 to allow the line to fully extend on the backcast.

5. Once the fly line is straight on the backcast, flex the rod forward and stop the rod at 10 o'clock.

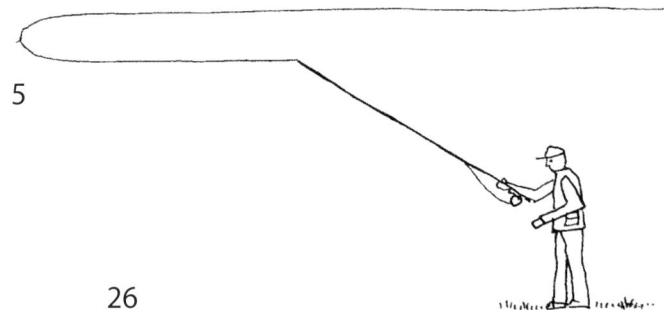

Basic Roll Cast

1. Like the overhead cast, start with the fly line straight and the rod tip touching the water.

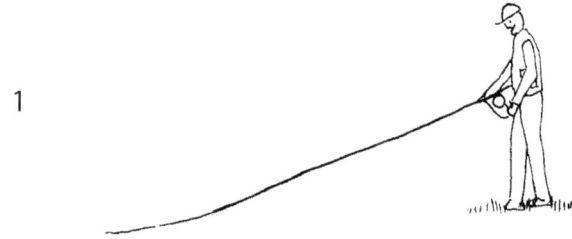

2. Begin slowly lifting the rod tip through the clockface, making sure to move the rod smoothly upwards and backwards.

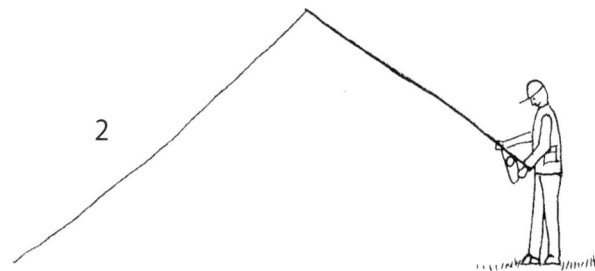

3. Once the rod is pointing at the 2 o'clock position, a loop of line hangs from the rod tip and touches the water - it's now time to do the forward cast.

4. With a quick 'flick' of the wrist, the rod is flexed forward and stopped sharply at the 10 o'clock position. The fly line then extends out and above the water.

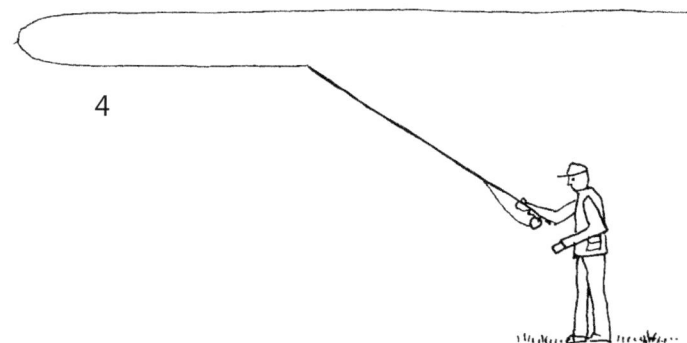

Little Grebe

The Little Grebe is one of the author's favourite riverside birds. Also Known as the Dabchick, this small bird inhabits slow moving waterways or lakes. If disturbed it will dive underwater and may emerge with only its head showing above the water until danger has passed.

Chapter Nine

How to Handle a Trout

How to Handle a Trout

Trout are cold-blooded fish and once landed, must be handled with great care whether you intend to return them safely to the lake or the river, or take home to eat.

The Golden Rules of Handling Fish:

1. Use a knotless net to land your fish. Never drag your fish up the lakeside or riverside banking - this removes the layer of mucus that protects the fish from infection.

2. Always wet your hands before handling a fish. Remember trout are cold-blooded - warm, dry hands on a trout's cold body can cause the fish a 'burning' pain and serious distress.

3. Never lift a trout out of the water by the tail or by placing a finger through the gills. Always cradle the trout gently in both hands when handling the fish and never squeeze the trout's belly.

4. If your trout is to be returned to the lake or river, the quicker the fish is carefully unhooked and gently placed in the water, the better for the well-being of the fish.

5. If the trout rolls onto its side when returned to the water, hold it gently upright until it regains the strength to swim away on its own.

6. Treat your trout with the greatest of respect. If you intend to keep your fish, or if the fish is badly hooked and bleeding from the gills, always dispatch as quickly as possible with a firm strike to the back of the head.

Mute Swan

The Mute Swan can often be found on rivers, streams and lakes. It can weigh as much as 10kg and has a wingspan of almost 2.5 metres. The Mute Swan is one of seven species of swan in the world and can be distinguished by its orange bill and long, curved neck.

Chapter Ten

Our Waterside Environment

Our Waterside Environment

Learning to fly fish is as much about enjoying and learning about our natural environment and the wildlife that surrounds us when we are on our rivers and lakes. As anglers we must maintain and protect our fishing environment so generations to come can enjoy our wonderful sport. By following our Young Anglers Code of Conduct you can help to protect the countryside and look after the future of angling.

Young Anglers Code of Conduct:

1. Never leave your litter or discarded leader by the river or lakeside - it can badly injure or even kill wildlife.

2. Take your litter home and remember to recycle all plastic bottles, aluminium cans and paper.

3. Never disturb nesting birds or animals on the riverbank or lakeside.

4. Look after the local plant life - avoid trampling on or uprooting wild flowers.

5. Always handle fish with the greatest of care before safely returning them to the water.

6. Always observe the angling and countryside regulations of your area.

Most importantly, have fun when fishing, respect other people using the waterside and respect the natural surroundings of your countryside.

Our Waterside Environment

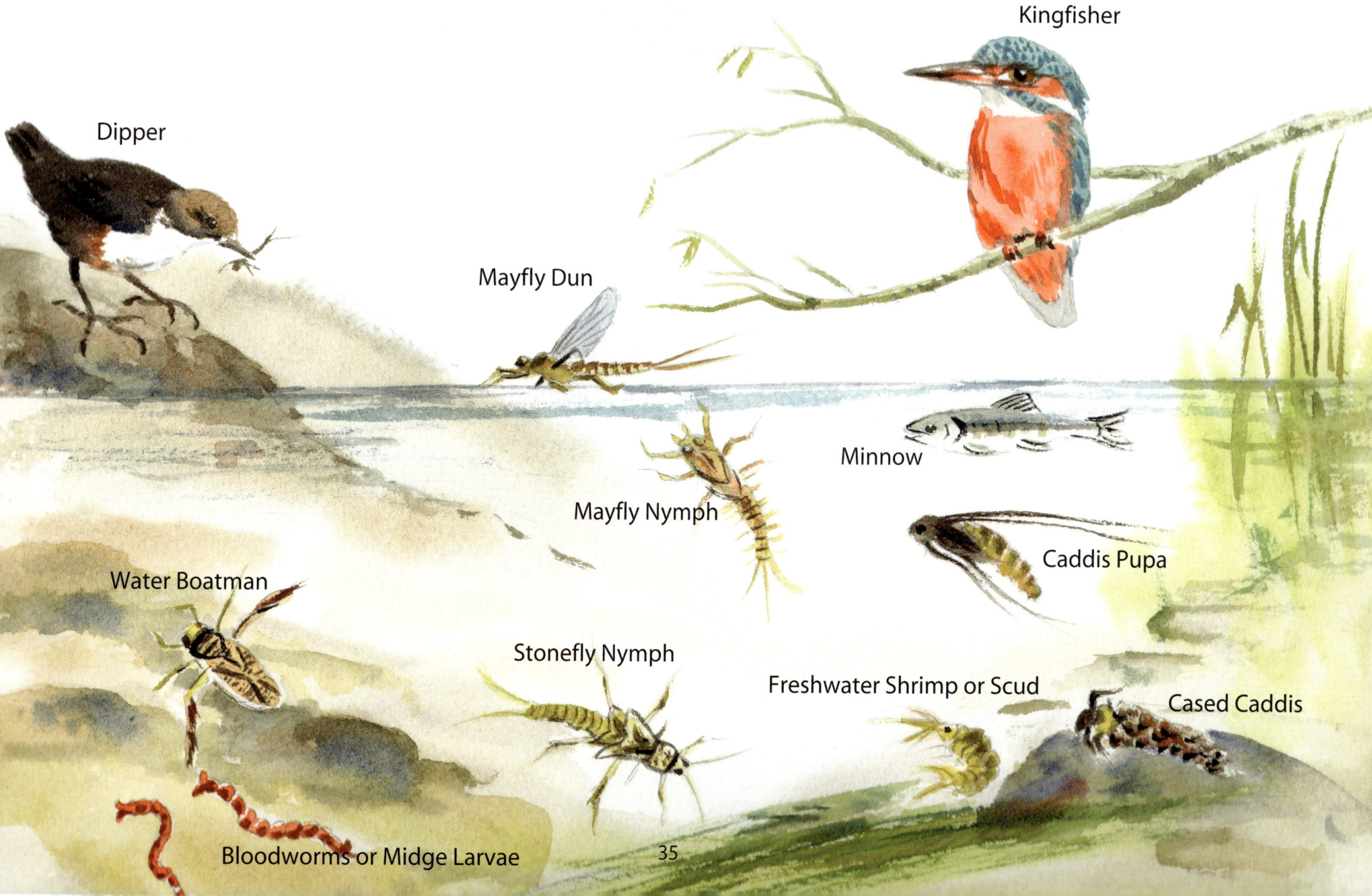

Kingfisher

Dipper

Mayfly Dun

Minnow

Mayfly Nymph

Caddis Pupa

Water Boatman

Stonefly Nymph

Freshwater Shrimp or Scud

Cased Caddis

Bloodworms or Midge Larvae

Buzzard

Although not a fish-eating bird, the buzzard can often
be seen soaring effortlessly over waterways. This
graceful bird has a wingspan of up to 130cm and can
be recognised by its distinct cat-like mewing call,
which it uses to define its territory.

Chapter Eleven

My Fishing Log

My Fishing Log

Date	Place	Type of Trout	Weight	Fly Pattern	Comments

Chapter Twelve

Word Search

Word Search

Can you answer these questions and find the words in the Word Search?

1. A very important item of safety equipment if you fall into the water. (10 letters)..

2. A trout is able to breathe oxygen through these. (5 letters)..

3. A small riverside bird that feeds on small fish. (10 letters)..

4. The large fin located on the trout's back used to keep the fish upright. (6 letters).......................................

5. The species of trout that takes its name from multi colours. (7 letters)..................................

6. An artificial fly is tied to the leader material with one of these. (4 Letters)...............................

7. A well known upwinged insect is often called this. (6 letters)....................................

8. A fly line is not only stored on one of these, it also helps to land a trout. (4 letters)...............................

9. The name of the young trout just before it becomes an adult. (4 letters).............................

10. When you learn to fly fish you must learn to do this. (4 letters)..............................

Answers:
1: Lifejacket. 2: Gills. 3: Kingfisher. 4: Dorsal. 5: Rainbow.
6: Knot. 7: Mayfly. 8: Reel. 9: Parr. 10: Cast